S0-BAP-135

BEING GRANDMA
AND GRANDPA

Grandparents Share Advice, Insights and Experiences

Emily Stier Adler and Michele Hoffnung

Grand Publications LLC

ISBN: 978-0-692-13223-4

Copy editing: Barbara Kuebke
Cover Design and art direction: Robin Lenowitz
Cover Image: © iStockPhoto.com

Marketing and publicity: Lucy Baker

Dedication

For our ten grandchildren: Arthur, David, Evan, Jeremy, Lalo, Nathan, Nicholas, Oscar, Pía, and Samuel

Contents

Introduction

We are grandmothers and social scientists (a sociologist and a developmental psychologist) who have published several books and many articles in our fields. Our combined experiences as grandmothers of 10 grandchildren span many years and stages of each of our lives -- first as full-time employed professionals, then through phased retirement and now mostly retired. We have seen our grandchildren through infancy and into adolescence; they range in age from newborn to 17. One of us lives reasonably close to two sets of grandchildren and both of us have grandchildren living several hundred miles away. We have frequent contact with our grandchildren and sometimes help with child care.

Some famous grandparents, such as Martha Stewart, Goldie Hawn, and Bill and Hillary Clinton,

1

pose with their grandchildren in various media. Others, such as journalist Leslie Stahl, write books about how delighted they are to be grandparents. But every day around the world, ordinary grandparents make a difference in the lives of their grandchildren and have grandchildren who make a difference in their lives.

We began this project to find out how grandparents who live independently and who are not the primary caretakers or custodians of their grandchildren see their roles and their relationships. We started with these questions: What are the joys and challenges of being a grandparent? How connected do grandparents feel to their children and grandchildren? How frequent is their contact with their grandchildren? How much help and advice do they give to their children and children-in-law? How do the relationships change over time? Do they use technology to keep in touch? Do their relationships with their grandchildren contribute to their own happiness? Do grandmothers and grandfathers see things differently? How do long-distance grandparents keep connected to their families?

We read many books and articles about grandparents. We focused on research about grandparents in gerontology, psychology and sociology and used it to inform our understanding of grandparenting today. We developed a set of questions about the grandparent experience and sent out a call for participation. We made numerous requests of grandparents and asked others to share the request with friends and family. We began talking to grandparents in July 2016 and finished in December 2017.

Many grandparents enthusiastically responded while others were more hesitant before agreeing to participate. We don't know how many women or men saw or heard about our project, but we do know that quite a few (dozens? hundreds?) declined to share their stories. More than twice as many women as men told us about their experiences. We don't know exactly why grandfathers did not respond as readily as grandmothers. We do know that men are typically less likely to respond to surveys than women and, more specifically, grandmothers are more likely to participate in social research than grandfathers. Studies tell us there is great variation among grandparents, with some being more involved in the role than others. Perhaps men are more private than women, are less engaged, or feel less adequate as grandparents. One grandfather who decided not to participate told us, "Well, I am not a very involved grandfather so figure I shouldn't be part of this project." Another said he tried to think about the issues, but was not able to get into participating. He said he could "understand why you do not have

3

as many grandfathers responding as it's not a guy thing." Whatever the reasons, fewer grandfathers than grandmothers participated.

Over the course of 17 months, we heard from 224 grandparents -- conversations in person, by phone and by email. We have no illusion that these grandparents are representative of all grandparents. We think they are probably more engaged and involved than "typical" grandparents. Grandparents who are less involved with their children and grandchildren are less likely to want to talk about their experiences. We also know that sharing your story with someone who may be a stranger means that some parts of the story are held back or are presented in the most positive light. The disappointing or painful parts of a life are often kept private.

While the grandparents who shared their views and experiences with us do not represent the full grandparenting spectrum, we appreciated hearing about the joys of being a grandparent as well as some of the disappointments. Those who took the time to share their wisdom with us have our gratitude.

4

In the following chapters we share parts of their stories and set them within the context of social research. We hope that grandparents will find it interesting and useful to see how others navigate the wonderful and sometimes challenging role of grandparent. We do not present blueprints for grandparenting, but rather advice and suggestions gleaned from the insights of grandparents, research data and our own experiences. We hope that readers will enjoy reading about grandparenting and how to be memorable grandparents.

CHAPTER 1

Grandparents Today

Mᵒʳᵉ than 70 million grandparents live in the United States, with more baby boomers joining their ranks every day. Most Americans age 65 and older have grandchildren; two-thirds have at least four. In Europe, grandparents have an average of about four grandchildren; English grandparents have an average of almost five. The majority of grandparents have separate residences; just one in 10 live with their grandchildren.

The grandparents who participated in our research had from one to 14 grandchildren, with an average of 3.8. Some were anticipating the birth of new grandbabies; others likely will in the future. So our information is a snapshot in time

The grandmothers and the grandfathers who told us their stories were on average 70 years old, with no difference in age between the genders. The grand-parents resided in 19 states, although more than half came from our home states of Massachusetts and Connecticut. Eleven participants lived in the United Kingdom or Canada.

Families used to be larger and life expectancy short-er. In the 19th cen-tury and before, families typically were composed of one or two genera-
tions, with many more individuals in each generation. Grandparents had more children and grandchildren, but typically knew them for fewer years. Now, with smaller families and longer lifespans, grandparents have fewer grandchildren but may live long enough to become great-grandparents. This type of family structure has been called "the beanpole family" be-cause it is "long" and "thin" -- a multi-generational extended family with several generations within the family but few siblings in each generation. Grand-parents generally occupy a central position in bean-pole families.

The timing of becoming a grandparent is impor-tant. Late middle age (50s to early 60s) is considered the "right time." Our participants were on average 58.5 years old when they first became grandparents. Very early grandparenthood often causes distress because it is likely to reflect off-time parenting on the part of a teenager or young-adult child, and pushes the new grandparent to feel prematurely old in our youth-oriented culture. It also increases the amount of support that grandparents are likely to provide for the children and grandchildren. Timing also has an impact on how available grandparents are for their grandchildren, as about half of all grandparents are employed full or part time. Some retire in order to spend more time helping their families, but others who retire have plans of their own. Many grandparents juggle multiple roles along with that of grandparent, including spouse, parent, parent-in-law, friend, community volunteer and labor-force participant.

Satisfaction with the grandparent experience

Becoming a grandparent is a source of happiness for most. Having raised their child with at least a fair amount of success, they now get to meet the next generation. In a self-selected survey of almost 5,000 grandparents, three-quarters told Grandparents. com that being a grandparent was the single most important and satisfying thing in life. In another survey, older Americans were asked whether they were experiencing the "good things" that can come with aging. Time with grandchildren was highly ranked, with almost a third saying that spending time with grandkids was what they valued most about getting older.

Almost all the grandparents who shared their stories with us were "very satisfied" and talked about the upsides of grandparenting. They described how much they enjoy interacting with grandchildren and how becoming a grandparent reinforced their connections to their adult children as they formed attachments to the newest generation.

We asked grandparents how frequently they saw grandchildren, how they kept in touch, what they felt was the best thing about being a grandparent, if being a grandparent contributed to their lives, and how connected they felt to their grandchildren. Two-thirds of the grandparents were very engaged in grandparenting, about a quarter were somewhat engaged and only 4 percent were disengaged from their grandchildren. Typical of their comments was that made by the grandfather who said, "They've added a lot of joy and fun to my life." Another declared, "Grandchildren clearly contribute to aging in a rich environment. They bring all of the joy of children but without the day-to-day responsibility and oversight. I can't imagine life without them now." Many would agree with the grandmother who said, "Being with them helps me live in the moment so I don't think of anything that's hassling me when I'm with them." Yet another noted that having youngsters in her life again kept her feeling young and connected to today's world through the warmth and joy of her grandchildren's love. The disappointment of those with less rewarding experiences as grandparents is reflected by the grandmother who said, "I have no pertinent advice to give anyone on either parenting or grandparenting. My grade average is an 'F'."

Given the social expectations that grandparenting will be rewarding and the self-selected nature of our sample, it is likely that grandparents with more negative experiences either chose not to talk about them or did not participate. We did, however, hear from a few with special needs grandchildren, including autism, Tourette Syndrome, behavioral problems and physical disabilities. Not surprisingly, this caused grandparents to worry for the grandchild and the adult parents. Nonetheless, in each case, the grandparent expressed love for the grandchild. And even for these grandparents, the positive feelings shine through. As one grandfather told us, "Grandparenting is one of the few things in life that is not overhyped."

The distance factor

Geographic mobility has a major influence on grandparenting. Young adults move away from home, marry and have children, and sometimes older adults relocate, most commonly when they retire. About four in 10 of the grandparents with whom we communicated had only "near" grandchildren (one or more living within 90 miles). About three in 10 had only "far" grandchildren (one or more living 90 or more miles away). The rest had both "near" and "far" grandkids. As one might expect, distance affects frequency of in-person visits. Nationally, the great majority of those whose grandchildren live nearby see them at least a few times a month, while half of those with grandchildren more than 100 miles away see them only two or three times a year. This was true for our grandparents as well, with in-person visits more common among those who live close to their grandchildren, although there were exceptions as evidenced by a few hardy grandparents who live 90 or more miles away but see their grandchildren at least every other week.

The frequency of visits with grandchildren varied widely -- from once a day to once a year. Grandparents who live nearby usually get to see grandchildren fairly often, but some far away grandparents spend weeks together with the grandchildren over summer and school vacations.

Grandparents providing child care

Grandparents living apart from grandchildren are often the major providers of non-parental, unpaid child care. In the United States, one-fifth of all preschoolers are cared for at least part time by grandparents, and almost two-thirds of grandparents provided a least some grandchild care over a 10-year period. For the great majority of American grandparents, however, child care is only an occasional responsibility, with about one-in-five saying they provided child care regularly.

Two-thirds of the grandmothers and grandfathers with whom we communicated provide child care for grandchildren or had done so at least occasionally in previous years. The amount of care varied greatly. Some committed to being the caretaker several hours

13

for some days; others did so for one or more days a week over the course of the year. One grandmother told us that she had 20 days on her calendar marked for child care for the first six months of the upcoming year because she cares for the grandchildren when their schools close for a half or full day. Some grandparents go to the grandchild's home for only a few days a year to help out; others take care of grandchildren during most school and summer vacations. Some grandmothers and grandfathers do child care individually; others help as a couple.

Although the great majority of grandparents told us they provide care willingly, we did hear of problems. Some feel taken for granted, their own needs not considered. One grandfather told us, "I don't want to feel like a 'doormat' and have the grandkids dumped on me every time they want to go somewhere. I think parents need to be sensitive to this. I'm the one who says 'no' to them more often – no candy, etc. I've noticed that my wife is more of the 'good cop' and won't deny them things." One grandmother who provides routine child care found that her children would sometimes tell her of schedule changes at the last minute, so she felt she had to cancel her own plans to accommodate their needs. Another, who had cared for her grandson two days a week for his first two years, had her regular child care canceled without any discussion. When she showed up at the door, she was told the child had been placed in a day-care center. A grandfather cautioned, "Set good boundaries and don't let your kids 'use' you as a built-in babysitter. Make sure you have your own life. You hopefully are more than a grandparent."

Grandparental age has an impact on the provision of child care, with the amount decreasing as grandparents age, in part because older grandparents have older grandchildren who do not need day care. In a national survey, 39 percent of American grandparents 65 and older said they have helped their adult children at least occasionally with child care in the past 12 months. Half of those in their 60s and early 70s, a third of those 75-84 and only a few of those over 85 say they helped with child care in the past year.

Grandparent roles

Grandparent roles can include caregiver, loving companion, family historian, transmitter of values, helper and mentor. Of course, a grandparent can play several or all of these roles. Grandparents told us about the ways they thought grandparents should behave. Almost half said it is most important to be a loving presence. One grandmother expressed

15

this by saying, "Grandchildren should always have someone in their lives from whom they can expect unconditional love and approval and attention. That's the grandparent's job description." Another noted, "Treasure their presence in your life and don't be afraid to let them know how much they mean to you. Saying 'I love you' at the end of visits and conversations is meaningful."

The second most common role that grandparents mentioned was as helper. Almost half told us they offer help to the grandchildren and their adult parents. One grandmother said, "Making time to play with the child helps establish the relationship and offers a chance to help the child develop skills. Grandparents can also help young or working parents by providing child care or driving children, which is practical and emotional aid." A grandfather noted, "Grandparents should be there to help out and provide a safety net if needed."

About one-fifth of the grandparents viewed teaching grandchildren or being a positive role model as most important. One grandmother commented, "The best thing about being a grandmother is watching the grandchildren grow through the various stages of life, and having some influence on their growth. I love to watch them learn to do things and teach them how to do things." In a similar vein, another said, "I spent time teaching them and giving them experiences they wouldn't get from their parents. My [art] teaching experience was shared with them." One grandmother focuses on teaching specific skills, noting, "Grandparents should use their talents and skills to enhance the lives of their grandchildren. For example, my husband and I are the cyclists in the family, so we taught our grandson how to ride a bike. I am crafty, so I spend a lot of time with my grandson on projects. I was proud to hear that his preschool teachers think he is very creative."

Others believe that grandparents should "tell the children of the history of everyone in their family and give  them a connection to the past." They talked about the importance of helping children learn values, saying things like, "They should teach as well as set an example. They should take children to church or synagogue. They should bake cookies for grandchildren and then bake cookies with grandchildren. They should be reliable and keep promises. They need to make sure grandchildren are taught accountability and responsibility." Some grandparents taught values and shared information about ethnic and religious heritage. One grandmother took her granddaughter to an after-school program at a Chinese cultural center. Another grandmother taught the value of charity on Thanksgiving. After the festive dinner each year she talked about being grateful for what one has and the importance of sharing with others. She then passed around information about charities that she had vetted and asked each child to pick one that spoke to him or her. The grandmother then donated money to the charities and had the newsletters sent to each child. One grandfather suggested the family join a group that held events to celebrate Korean adoptees' heritage and also cooked Korean food for Sunday family dinners.

Also important to grandparents is their role as "supporter" or "cheerleader" for grandchildren. One fifth made comments like, "Praise your grandchild for both big and small accomplishments. Always focus on the child's behavior in a positive way, commenting on what a good job he or she did." Said another, "Be a sounding board for them. They don't want to discuss some things with their parents so let them know we've been down this road before. Same scenario, different players -- assure them that it will be all right." Another said, "Grandparents should show their grandchildren all the positives in life --

good relationships, enjoyable travel, balanced diets. They should never speak negatively about their parents" or, another added, "of the other grandparents."

Some grandparents advised "just enjoy" grandchildren and their activities. One grandparent noted, "Enjoy every minute you have with them because the years go by at triple the rate you experienced with your own children." Another said, "We enjoy being a part of their lives, whether being invited to piano performances, plays, swim meets, soccer games, etc. Our presence signifies quiet support to them."

Fewer than one in 10 said grandparents should give help by providing money for educational funds or to help the parents afford activities for the grandchildren. The emphasis clearly was on giving time and love.

Grandparents are thoughtful and active people. They help children and grandchildren and try hard to connect with them in a variety of ways. They enjoy their time with grandchildren and for the most part are satisfied with the roles they play in the family. And as we will discuss in the chapters that follow, the role of grandparent is not static. Families are not all the same when grandchildren enter the picture and they all change over time, as the younger generation develops and adult generations age.

CHAPTER 2

Variations in the Grandparenting Experience

G randparenthood is a complex and diverse experience. The grandparents we talked to differed
in a variety of ways. Some are new grandparents,
with only a single infant grandchild; others have been
grandparents for two or more decades. Some have a
single set of grandchildren via only one child, others have several. Some live near their grandchildren;
others live far away. Some are "step" grandparents.
In this chapter we describe how differences influence
the experience of grandparenting.

Near or Far

The great majority of grandparents told us they feel connected with their grandchildren, but there were some differences between the local and more geographically distant grandparents. Most grandparents whose grandchildren live nearby feel very connected with them. On the other hand, just over half of those who only have grandchildren living more than 90 miles away feel very connected.

But geography is not destiny. Several described greater closeness with a long-distance family than with a nearby one. "Because of the personalities of the parents, I feel most connected to the children of our third son, even though they are the farthest away," one grandmother said. "They openly encourage a close relationship with me/us. I keep in touch with them at least twice a week on FaceTime, and generally know what is going on in their lives. My son and his wife both encourage this. My son is a great housekeeper, baker and cook, and often calls me for advice in that regard, so I have quite a different relationship with him than I do with the other two [sons]." A grandfather said, "Kind of ironic -- I'm closer to the two households far away than I am to the two close by." Distance matters, but it does not determine connection, closeness or being a hands-on grandparent. And sometimes close is too close, as with the grandfather who told us about the grandchild who lives only one flight of stairs away and pops in several times a day, which was too much for him.

Distance matters when it comes to providing child care. One study found that 60 percent of those who lived within an hour of the grandchildren are currently or have previously provided child care for grandchildren under age 13 while parents were at work or school. Of those providing child care, just over half provided care less than 12 hours per week; the rest did more.

Distance matters to our grandparents as well. Our "nearby" grandparents provide significantly more care than those with at least some grandchildren "far away." But even grandparents who live far from all grandchildren provide some care. A few even drive an hour or two to spend one or two days a week caring for grandchildren. Overall, "nearby" ones are more likely to have regular child-care days, whereas long-distance ones are more likely to help when they

23

are visiting or when they are called in for special circumstances, such as parents taking a vacation, the birth of another child, or a medical crisis. One long-distance grandmother of a 7-month-old described it this way: "When we go to their house, we usually are providing day care and will take the baby out for walks, hikes, park, swings and slides and other outdoor activities. My husband has gone to the pool with our granddaughter. We feel quite connected as we have shared coverage of day care since she was born. My husband and I have taken turns to watch our granddaughter for seven weeks over the past six months. Since we are staying at their house, we see our granddaughter 24/7 when we are in there." That last is an important point. One grandfather estimated that he spends as much time with his long-distance grandchildren as his nearby ones because the visits are longer and round the clock, though less frequent. That is highlighted by another grandmother who said, "I spent weeks and even an entire month being his 'nanny' when the family lived 3,000 miles away."

Blended families

Divorce among parents and grandparents some-times can lead to complicated relationships. Some grandchildren of those in our study had six or eight grandparents. One grandmother, remarried for decades, told us that her husband is not very connected to her children or grandchildren. Another noted that her divorced children are non-custodial parents, which limits her interaction with her grandchildren. Both grandfathers and grandmothers spoke of helping single parents with child care after divorce. Others happily welcomed step-grandchildren into their hearts. One mentioned, "I have two that are step-grandchildren, which I consider as my grandchildren, a gift of two that I love."

Step-grandchildren/grandparent relationships are diverse. Some longterm step-grandparents were step-parents to the generation in between, making the connection organic. As one grandfather put it, "I am very connected to all six grandchildren. I consider them my flesh and blood, although two of my children are step rather than blood (it don't make no diff)." Other step-grandparents married a biological grandparent after the generation in between had left home. They become step-grandparents when the grandchildren are born, without having been stepparents. These have been called skip-generation grandparents, because they skipped the in-between generation. Skip-generation relationships depend upon how grandparents act, the warmth of the relationships between parents and steps, and whether the parents facilitate the step-grandchild/step-grandparent relationship.

We spoke to grandparents who feel close to their step-grandchildren and others who do not. One grandfather, whose 14 grandchildren include step-grandchildren, said, "Some of the grandkids are what one would call 'step-grandkids' although that term is rarely if ever used. All the kids were born after our marriage so they have always known us as their grandparents." A grandmother said, "I have known him since he was born and have always been his 'grandma.'" Another grandfather described very good connections with his two grandchildren even though he is "a step-grandfather inasmuch as my wife is a late marriage with a grown daughter." On the other hand, one grandmother said, "We have two step-grandchildren, boys 8 and 10, who became part of our family two years ago, when my oldest daughter married. The boys have two sets of active grandparents and so we asked them to call us aunt and uncle. Because they already have solid, good relationships with their grandparents, we are merely visiting relatives or their step-mom's parents." Similarly, a grandmother whose daughter has blended a family of her two children and her husband's one made it clear that she considers only her daughter's natural children to be her grandchildren. In contrast, another grandmother explained that she carefully embraced all as her grandchildren because her own mother-in-law had caused a lot of pain by treating the sons born to her first marriage as not part of their family.

Special needs

Although virtually all grandparents we talked to described their experiences in highly positive ways, those with special needs grandchildren, including those with autism, Tourette's, behavioral problems and physical disabilities, had extra worries both for the grandchild and the adult parents. Almost all said they try to be as helpful as possible, to support the parents and to provide advice and assistance. Our findings are consistent with the relatively few studies of grandparents with special needs grandchildren, which indicate that grandparents usually provide support, with the support generally valued by parents. As with typically developing grandchildren, grandparents bring four types of basic resources to the families: experience, time, access to various kinds of instrumental support, and financial resources.

Grandparents with grandchildren on the autism spectrum, for example, are often part of the family's support network and provide emotional support, financial support, respite care, transportation to and from appointments, and advocacy within schools and the broader community. Despite the challenges, grandparents tell of the joys they experience with grandchildren on the autism spectrum.

Grandparents we spoke with frequently made helpful interventions. Sometimes this was difficult, as when a grandmother noticed that her two-year-old grandson did not make eye contact with her. This led to unpleasant interactions with the parents, who had no previous experience with children and thought their own child was perfect. With persuasion and financial assistance, the grandparents helped their autistic grandchild get diagnosis and treatment. This grandmother was one of several who told of identifying developmental delays and urging parents to seek professional attention. One grandmother said, "My only granddaughter is my daughter's only child; all three of us are very close to each other. My daughter is a magnificent mother and has always accepted my husband's and my suggestions and advice with grace. We worried about her daughter's late speech development and late reading -- she caught up completely,

28

but our daughter took our advice about testing and was patient with our concerns."

Another said, "I try not to give advice unless asked but have brought attention in three of the families to the fact that their children have had some behaviors that were not of the norm for their ages and urged that they seek help. Some believed me right away and sought help and had good results. Others were initially disbelieving of what I mentioned for at least several years and got help later than I thought they should. My family has a history of mental illness so I have been very conscious of aberrant behavior and alcoholism." One grandfather voiced what was noted by several: "The only negative to being a grandparent is you have more extremely important people to worry about." Nonetheless, in each case the grandparent expressed love for the grandchild and provided important support to the parents which indirectly benefited the grandchild.

Adoption

Another variation is when children or grand-children have been adopted. A mother of two ad-opted children found special pleasure in her grand-children. "I feel really blessed because both my children are adopted and I would never have had the

joy of grandkids if it wasn't for them in my life. I got the added joy of watching them see for the first time someone that looked like them with the birth of their children."

Only three mentioned that grandchildren were adopted (although we know that several others have adopted grandchildren). They spoke of their grandchildren without distinction as to how they entered their family and in ways similar to other grandparents. Those who mentioned it always referred to an international adoption, often in the context of describing variety, such as, "I am the lucky grandparent of 12 grandchildren, who are scattered from Massachusetts to New Jersey to Maryland. Two grandsons live in Connecticut, about 20 minutes away. Six grandkids are male and six are female. In that group are twin girls, age 13, a grandson adopted from Bolivia, and a grandson with autism."

Three grandparents mentioned that their own children were adopted. One mentioned that one of his children had been put up for adoption. Each of those events appeared to be more dramatic in their lives than whether a grandchild was adopted. As one put it, "We have three children, all adopted. They are bio siblings whom we adopted at the same time from Russia (in 1994). Only the younger daughter has a child, which has brought us closer. With the birth of our granddaughter, we definitely got the baby experience for the first time."

Whether the grandchildren come into the family by birth, adoption or marriage, whether they live far or near, or whether they are typically developing or not, the key to satisfying grandparent/grandchild relationships is the quality of relationships with adult children and their partners. As one grandmother put it, "The people 'in charge' of your grandchildren are their parents. The parents are the 'gatekeepers' of the children. The frequency and quality of the visits are determined by them. It is delusional (really) to think that one can have a good, close relationship with one's grandchildren if there is tension or conflict with one's adult children and/or their partners. Advice would be to work out those relationships on an ongoing basis, keeping those relationships loving. That will ensure access to one's grandkids." It is to these intergenerational relationships we next turn.

What's a Grandparent to Do?

Don't expect a story book relationship with your grandchildren. Your adult children will make choices that have little to do with you. These choices will have implications for your grandparenting experience. For some, this may mean more of or fewer grandchildren than expected. For others, it may mean "far away" grandchildren. Remember, you do not get to make their decisions, but you do get to choose your responses.

Distance is not a barrier to emotional closeness. It is easier to see "near" grandchildren than "far away" ones, but the nature of the relationships you have with their parents is likely to have a major impact on whether you feel close or not.

Be welcoming to all grandchildren. Welcome each new addition to the family, so you can enjoy the benefits of warm relationships with grandchildren. Families are complex, and helping members blend smoothly is in everyone's interest.

Provide as much help as you can for special-needs grandchildren and their parents. But whether a grandchild is typically developing or special needs, grandparent help should be coordinated with the parents.

Adoption and remarriage are not barriers. *Grandparent bonds do not depend upon blood ties. Form warm connections with grandchildren, regardless of how they come your way.*

CHAPTER 3

The Generation in Between

Grandparents are usually happy being grand-parents and find satisfaction in their roles and relationships. Most, however, need to adjust to the realization that as grandparents they are not in control of all family situations. As one grandmother told us, "The worst thing about being a grandparent is not having the final say as to how your grandchild is raised -- setting the rules and discipline, etc. You love them like your own, but do not have that control."

Although the grandchild/grandparent bond is one of the three relationships that represent the basic intergenerational triangle of the family, the most critical one is the parent/child bond. Grandparents usually recognize that their children are adults and, as such, they must let go and allow them to be independent and autonomous and decide how to raise the grandchildren. They understand the differences between roles of the parent and grandparent and want to respect the parent/child bond, but they also want their grandchildren to "turn out right."

More than one-third of grandparents we talked to volunteered that they recognize that they are not principally responsible for the upbringing of their grandchildren and that they do not want to undermine the parents' authority. They may cringe at parental standards of housekeeping, household food, media use, discipline and the like, but they tend to keep quiet. One grandmother noted, "I had my chance to make my own mistakes with my children." Another commented that "we did it our way as parents and now it's their turn." One grandfather was more specific: "The parents' values may differ from ours -- and it could be generational. I don't believe it's appropriate to try and overlay my values on their children. Times are different. My opinion is not better than their opinion."

Relationships with adult children

Grandparents noted that the relationships they have with their own children and children-in-law are especially important as they strive for good rela-

tionships with grand-
children. Parents are
the mediators or con-
duits between grand-
parents and grandchil-
dren and can foster
or obstruct these re-
lationships. Grandparents learn quickly that they need
to negotiate with the generation in between to connect
with their grandchildren. One grandmother was explicit
when she said, "Kids these days have a lot of power over
us and it would be dreadful to be shut out."

Parents, especially new ones, have strong preferences for the kinds of interactions they want with
their own parents. They recognize that grandparents
are a major source of advice and support when a baby
is born and appreciate their help. A survey of British
adults, for example, found that grandparents were
seen as very important in ensuring the well-being of
children. When asked to identify up to three people
or organizations that were the most supportive when
they had a baby, almost two-thirds of parents rated
their mother or father as the most important. New
parents want supportive communication, including
positive shared feelings and information, as well as
concrete examples of assistance, such as gifts and
shared celebrations. Such forms of interaction can

be helpful in building intergenerational relationships, but critical and unsolicited advice can have negative effects.

Differing expectations regarding the grandparent role sometimes lead to ambivalent feelings. Grandparents often feel they are supposed to follow two potentially contradictory cultural norms: "being there" and "not interfering." For some, "being there" means providing support when their children request it but not being "pushy" about it, which would be seen as interfering. For others, "being there" means being involved with, invested in and connected with grandchildren. However, the ways grandparents are involved are affected by their life circumstances, including material resources, proximity and health. Competing expectations can result in both positive and negative feelings, such as affection and resentment.

Advice given and withheld

The grandparent mantras shared with us were "be loving," "be supportive" and "enjoy the grandchildren." Grandparents want to "be there" when they are needed. For some, this means physical help, such as providing child care; for others it is emotional and psychological support. And for some it is financial

assistance. Only a bit more than one in 10 told us they at least occasionally give unsolicited advice to their children about parenting styles and strategies. The rest said that they never criticize or give advice unless asked. A few hedged by saying things like, "We stay out of the advice-giving business and would only do so if the situation was critical." Others said they offer advice only if they feel the parents will be receptive. One grandmother said that one of the few times she gave advice was when the parents of her grandchildren complained that the youngest would wake in the night and demand that mom or dad sleep near the bed. This disrupted the parents' sleep. The grandmother suggested that an older sibling sleep in the room with the younger one. This suggestion was accepted and, because it worked, the grandmother was a hero for the moment.

A few grandparents talked about having discussions rather than giving advice. "I never give unsolicited advice," one said, "but I've enjoyed the many conversations I've had with them about parenting, in which they often ask for my take on things." Another said, "I've talked them through many situations in their lives." Still others commented that rather than give advice, they might ask questions of the parents about how things could be handled.

Grandparents know there can be negative consequences for unsolicited advice- giving, for interfering or for rejecting parental instructions. One grandmother remarked that when her first grandchild was a toddler, her heart hurt when the toddler cried because of parental discipline. The grandmother said she would intercede to try to "make it better" for the child until she realized the parents were not happy about that. When her son said, "It's okay for him to cry because we said no and you should stay out of it," the grandmother learned to turn a deaf ear to the child's cries. Another grandmother told this story: "My son said to me, 'Mom, I'm going to show you how to change a diaper.' I almost laughed but my answer was 'Thank you.' I'm trying to be non-judgmental, supportive and encouraging."

Our grandparents were almost unanimous in giving similar -- and succinct – advice: "Don't interfere." "Mind your business." "Never criticize." "Don't meddle." "Don't show disapproval." "Zip your lip." "Never push your agenda." "Don't butt in." "Understand boundaries." "Don't overstep limits." "Understand your role as a secondary helper." "Walk on eggshells." Quipped one, "I don't know how grandparents are able to talk because we spend

most of the time biting our tongues!" These suggestions were best summed up by the grandmother who
said, "Walk softly and carry a big heart."

Daughters and sons

The quality of the grandparent/grandchild relationship is affected by the quality of the grandparent/
parent relationship. Grandparents who have rapport
with a child are more likely to be involved with the
grandchild as well. One grandmother told us that
she is emotionally close to her son and has enjoyed
phone conversations with him several times a week
since his graduation from college. When he became
a father, this son included his parents in his children's
lives with visits, phone calls and video chats, which
have enabled them to connect to the grandchildren.

Just 10 of the grandparents we talked to have
children who are single parents. Overall, the
grandparents had almost equal numbers of sons
and daughters who are parents of their grandchildren. According to some social science research,
grandparents have a hierarchy of feelings for the
parents of their grandchildren, with grandparents
most connected with daughters, then sons, then
sons-in-law and lastly daughters-in-law. Most of the
grandparents we talked to did not tell us of a favorite

41

child. The few who did were about equally divided between sons and daughters. Some did note being closer to their children than to their children-in-law. When describing their in-law children, however, the great majority of grandparents reported that they like them. One grandmother said, "I have been very lucky to always feel welcome and appreciated by both my adult children and their spouses, so being in their homes with my grandchildren is wonderful." Another told us that "we are very, very lucky, and we have warm, close relationships with our children and their spouses. We have a wonderful time when we are all together." Some talked about sons-in-law very positively, saying things like, "My son-in-law is a delight and we interact all the time" and "He is very appreciative and respectful." Daughters-in-law were often lauded as well. The biggest compliment grandmothers gave was that an in-law child was like their own child. As one said, "I love her so much. She is always kind and loving to us. She is like a bonus daughter." Another commented, "I am blessed with excellent relationships with my sons and daughters-in-law. I know I can say anything to them and talk to them whenever I want. I consider my daughters-in-law to be like daughters."

Some grandparents did report a difficult relationship with at least one of their own children or with an in-law child. One grandmother said, "My relationship with my sons and my daughters-in-law can be described as civil and maybe 'duty bound.'" Another described her daughter as self-involved and confrontational.

One in five grandparents have at least a somewhat difficult relationship with at least one in-law child, but only a few more cited problems with daughters-in-law compared to sons-in-law. For some it was a lack of emotional intimacy with the daughter-in-law. For others, it was a sense that they play second fiddle to the daughter-in-law's mother. One grandmother said about her daughter-in-law, "When we are together, all is fine on the surface but I do not know how to interact with her." Another commented that "with daughters-in-law you need to watch what you say. I learned this very quickly and now I keep my nose out of things." Said another, "We have a loving relationship as long as we don't step out of line. My daughter-in-law runs the show and my son doesn't intervene." One described a daughter-in-law who "talks to me and tells me about the children, but I hear her give all the details to her own mother." One grandfather reported that the "mother-in-law/daughter-in-law dynamics are strained, and even for me our daughter-in-law is not an overtly relaxing person."

Problems with sons-in-law were also shared. One grandmother reported that her son-in-law often mocks her. Another labeled her son-in-law as a very difficult person and third said, "I have a complicated relationship with my son-in-law because he has very intense ups and downs." A grandfather noted that "my relationships with my three sons-in-law are very reserved and all family interaction is done through my daughters."

Even if there are complaints about a lack of closeness or warmth, if the child-in-law is a 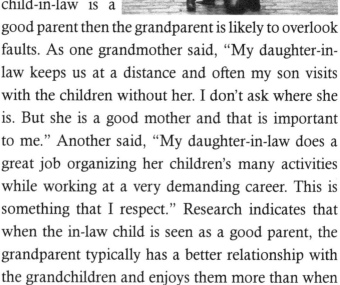 good parent then the grandparent is likely to overlook faults. As one grandmother said, "My daughter-in-law keeps us at a distance and often my son visits with the children without her. I don't ask where she is. But she is a good mother and that is important to me." Another said, "My daughter-in-law does a great job organizing her children's many activities while working at a very demanding career. This is something that I respect." Research indicates that when the in-law child is seen as a good parent, the grandparent typically has a better relationship with the grandchildren and enjoys them more than when the grandparent thinks the in-law child lacks parenting skills. But regardless of the skills and abilities of their children and in-law children, grandparents usually do what is necessary to get along. Grandparents told us that they work on the relationships because their children and in-law children are "gatekeepers." One grandmother specifically advised grandparents to maintain harmony with the parents to keep open the "door" to the grandchildren.

Becoming a grandparent can bring a person closer to the parental generation. Quite a few commented that it is wonderful to watch their child evolve. One grandfather said, "The best thing about being a grandfather is seeing my son become a fuller adult as a parent." Grandmothers said similar things: "My favorite thing about being a grandmother is watching my daughter be an amazing mother." "The best thing is watching my daughter as a parent. She is caring, loving, responsible, tuned to the children's needs, available and unconditionally loves her three children." "Seeing my son grow into this wonderful new role as father is a great pleasure. He is taking such kind, wonderful, joyful care of his daughter." A few grandparents commented that the new family bonds or participation in child care brought them closer to their children and children-in-law.

Family relationships change over time. As grandchildren grow up and grandparents grow older, the needs of both generations change. When grandchildren become older, they negotiate their own relationships with grandparents. We discuss the changes over time in Chapter 4.

What's a Grandparent to Do?

Mend family fences. *If there are conflicts or problems between you and your children or your children-in-law, make every effort to resolve them as soon as possible. Be willing to apologize for past behaviors and to let go of past grievances. These are your grandchildren's parents, so be kind to them.*

Remember that you don't set the rules. *Your children and in-law children are in charge, so be gracious and accept their authority.*

Don't be critical or give advice unless you are asked. *Although you may disagree with parental standards of housekeeping, child rearing and the like, unless there is a safety issue, don't butt in. Silence is usually appreciated more than*

46

advice. Participate in discussions that parents or grandchildren initiate.

Don't expect total family access and instant intimacy with your adult children, in-law children or grandchildren. *It's great if you have those kinds of relationships, but if you don't, respect their boundaries and privacy.*

Compliment the good things. *New parents are often unsure whether they are doing a good job. Encourage them by commenting on the things you believe they are doing right. Positive reinforcement helps new parents feel more secure as they find their way and can help build intergenerational bonds.*

Ask your children what kinds of help they want. *Be as generous with your time and money as you feel is appropriate but don't overwhelm the parents and grandchildren with gifts and offers.*

Help choose your name. *You will be called Grandma, Nana, Mimi, Granddad, Pop, etc. for many years. Make sure it's a name you like and are comfortable responding to. Decide on*

47

a name very early because your children and children-in-law may refer to you by your grandparental name before your grandchild speaks.

CHAPTER 4

Grandchildren Growing and Changing

G randparenting, like parenting, requires adjusting to the developmental needs of growing and changing youngsters. While infants and toddlers need constant child care, the hours decrease steadily as grandchildren start day care, preschool, and then school. As grandchildren mature, they spend more time in extracurricular activities and with friends. Although they still need supervision, it is different from when they were younger. Grandparents of school-aged children mentioned activities such as helping with homework, discussing interests, books and movies, and providing transportation. As one grandmother said after spending a week with her two teenaged grandsons, "Lots of cooking and mucho, mucho car rides."

Some of our participants miss the types of interaction they had when their grandchildren were younger. One said that "it was more fun when they were younger!" Another lamented, "When the children were younger they had more time for visits. Now they are SO busy with activities and schoolwork, they have no time for much else. Therefore [it is] worse."

Specific complaints typically involved friends, activities and media. One grandmother told of driving for six hours in order to arrive at her grandsons' house when they got home from school -- only to have them say hi, hand her their backpacks and tell her they would be back for dinner after playing with their friends across the street. She was especially sad that there were no hugs. A grandfather bemoaned, "I have always felt very connected to them, but as they have grown older, they seem to spend all their time on their computers. (They each have a PC and an iPhone -- internet only.) It is a rare occasion when we can sit down together and play a game. Even when we are having dinner together, they pay more attention to their phones. When I am watching them, they are always on the computer."

Others appreciate the changes. One grandmother concluded, "I can't say it's better or worse, but it is different." Another noted that interaction is less frequent now because her granddaughter has her own life, but it is not worse. One commented, "The relationship with the grandkids has changed only in that I can't spend hours reading to them or lying in bed with them and telling stories. Instead we hang out on the sofa and talk about music and movies and books and life -- not a bad exchange at all!" A long-distance grandmother saw several benefits to the grandchildren getting more mature: "As they grow up, they have more things to do, like sports, so they are more on the go. But we are able to connect faster, because they are more mature. The little, far-away ones will soon be able to fly here on their own, which will be great."

Other grandpar-ents made no judg-ment but said they understand that things change. "As they get older they have less  time to spend with their own parents, let alone me," one said. As the grandmother of a 17-year-old detailed, "The activities have changed as she grew. From age 2 or 3 to about 7 or 8, we went to the playground, read aloud, played in the backyard, had talks, had meals together. From age 8 to about 12, we helped with homework, made dinner at home, went to movies or museums on occasion. From 12 on, we have taken trips -- to Europe and Boston -- had meals or walks and talks. We sometimes drive her from one place to another and that is a time for talking. The frequency and involvement has decreased during the years, but in a way that is consistent with her levels of development. She is more focused on her grandparents and more willing to make time to get together than some grandchildren, or than we were with our own grandparents." This last point is insightful, because many current grandparents shared their grandparents with lots of cousins and had more formal relationships with them than our participants described. The grand-mother is also echoing studies showing that although adolescents spend less time with their grandparents, they continue to feel emotionally close to them. With current lifespans and communication patterns, to-day's grandchildren often have more years and better quality interactions with their grandparents.

Changing grandparental influence

Active grandparents, whether by birth, adoption or marriage, have influence. In chapter 3, we concluded that almost all grandparents agree with the rule of nonintervention. Even so, grandparents can sway and guide their children and grandchildren.

We heard of grandmothers serving as advocates for or advisors to their grandchildren. One told of caring for her infant grandson on a weekly basis. When her son wrote a magazine article about new parenting, he mentioned how surprised he was to come home from work to see the baby sitting in an infant seat happily inspecting his hand or some hanging object, while grandma was reading nearby. The grandmother explained that infants need some time on their own. In his desire to give enough attention to his baby, the new father had not considered that.

Indirect influence can take the form of giving advice, providing information, suggesting other ways of doing things, and modeling parenting skills. Direct influence is most frequent with teenagers, who may be developmentally at odds and in conflict with their parents. Involved grandparents can provide guidance to both the teens and their parents. One grandmother told of witnessing loud arguments between her teenage grandson and his father (her son). She tried to cool down both and then discussed the interaction with each of them separately. While many grandparents would not intervene so actively, it is often possible to discuss issues with a grandchild and/or

53

 adult child after the crisis is over.

A grandfather whose grandson was having academic problems offered to tutor him in an effort to ease conflict with the parents. Even with younger grandchildren, several respondents said they have privately suggested alternate parenting methods. This works best when the parents know that the grandparents are supportive and not judgmental of their parenting. Emotional closeness between parents and grandparents is associated with emotional closeness between grandchildren and grandparents.

Changing ways of connecting

When grandchildren are very young, grandparents prefer in-person visits, but they supplement them with other contact. FaceTime and Skype, especially if the grandchildren live at a distance, are used extensively. One grandmother described how much she likes using technology to interact. "We FaceTime once a week. My daughter-in-law and son send photos many times a week and also keep us abreast of her development -- crawling, babbling, activities. So glad I am living in this era of these modes of communication. When my children were young we also lived very far away from [their] grandparents and sent videotapes and photographs in the mail once or twice a year. This is amazing to be able to see our granddaughter so often and follow her development."

Many mentioned that use of technology depends on the age of the grandchildren. One said, "When they were little we did Skype so they would know who we are and we could see them growing up." Grandparents mentioned reading stories, using puppets, telling jokes or otherwise interacting with youngsters via video chats, before the kids outgrew them. One grandfather put on funny hats and "Groucho Marx" glasses and mustaches to make the toddlers laugh. But once kids get older, they often do not want to sit still and talk. One grandparent said, "FaceTime is now only really wanted by the 3-year-old. The other two have sort of "aged out" of the desire to speak/ interact with us some of the time."

One grandfather of 5-year-, 3-year- and 9-month-old grandchildren explained the changes he has experienced: "The most common medium is Face-Time. The older two, especially the oldest, aren't into it as much as when they were younger (not just with us, but with their other grandparents and cousins as well). When they get home after day care, they are more interested in imaginative play and letting off steam. We FaceTime most often with our daughter and the baby before the others wake up; that has been a really sweet way to nurture our relationship with our grandson, given that he is so young he might otherwise lose the connection with us between visits. We also text-message with the parents, and with texts we often get pictures and videos of things they are doing. We email as well. So we do get a fair amount of contact, but it can be a bit erratic when they are in a busy stretch."

For older grandchildren, taking them out, especially one-on-one, is a way to stay connected. For example, a woman with four granddaughters said she started taking each one to lunch (sometimes adding a shopping spree) a few times a year when they were in their teens and has continued the tradition even though all are now in their twenties.

For connecting remotely, texting or joining grandchildren on social media can work, sometimes with restrictions. One grandmother explained that all her grandchildren have "friended" her on Facebook -- with instructions about what she can and cannot do: no posting photos of them and no commenting on pictures of them. Grandparents who are comfortable with smart phones and able to text and send links to things of mutual interest do so. Many mentioned that their grandchildren prefer texts, although grandparent preferences differed. One noted, "I would rather see them in person! I also prefer a phone conversation but understand it is much more likely to be texting back and forth, often with photos, and I have adjusted to the times!" Another commented, "Not much use of the phone for any of them now. When they were younger they all did. And now they never use email." Some grandparents, however, are not happy with texting. Said one grandmother, "I have a flip phone, so texting is not easy. I don't even like texting!" Another commented, "It's ok if you know how to!"

We found a gender gap in the use of electronic devices; significantly more grandfathers than grandmothers use electronic means to connect with children and grandchildren. Among married grandparents, the electronic connection is in the interest of the couple, but more women than men depend upon their spouse to make this connection. One grandmother told us, "Grandkids are not phone talkers yet. My husband checks social media accounts occasionally but I don't." Another noted, "We use phone, text and cards, and my husband uses social media." Yet another said, "I telephone. My husband is better with email and text." This leads to our discussion of whether gender matters in the grandparent experience.

What's a Grandparent to Do?

Expect changes as the grandchildren develop. *Babies need care 24/7; teenagers need help with homework and rides; adult grandchildren need counsel. Adjust your expectations and interactions to their age level.*

Remain aware that you do not have control. As they age, continue to respect the rule of nonintervention. Discuss options, if that is something the family does, but respect parental authority.

Be aware that you have indirect influence. Your behavior serves as a model for the parents and the grandchildren, and your suggestions may as well. Serve as a good and loving model.

You may have direct influence with teenage grandchildren. When teenagers are at odds with their parents, a trusted grandparent may be asked for advice or information. Be there for them.

Staying connected requires flexibility. *Babies typically stay in one place. If their parents are willing, you can visit them in person or on FaceTime or Skype. Older children are busy with school, friends and activities. Use whatever method they prefer to stay connected.*

Technology can help keep the generations in touch*. Sending texts, using apps and social media can help you keep in touch when "old-fashioned" ways do not. Be open to new technology. Ask your grandchildren to help you learn what you need to use it.*

CHAPTER 5

Does Gender Matter?

As gender roles have evolved, so have the activities of grandfathers and grandmothers. For the most part, women still are expected to care for and connect with children, but modern views of masculinity now encourage men to be nurturing and expressive. This led us to consider the current importance of gender in grandparenting.

Many contemporary grandfathers have been active and engaged fathers. As a result, connecting with grandchildren is  well within their expertise and expectation. Other grandfathers became interested in engaging when grandchildren came along. As one grandmother noted, "My ex-husband is a better grandfather than he was a father." In addition, as is typical of the "bean-pole" family, most of today's extended families have fewer siblings per generation, but more generations. With fewer aunts and uncles in extended kinship groups, some grandfathers have taken over more family roles, including more active involvement with grandchildren.

Studies of grandfathers are rare, but a small project found them to be active participants in their families, behaving in ways that did not support stereotypical images of passive, remote and disengaged grandfathers. Instead, most of these grandfathers had loving relationships with their grandchildren. Studies of grandparents that compare genders note that while both take care of grandchildren, grandmothers spend more time than grandfathers providing care. In Australia, for example, in a study of more than 300 grandparents with 1-year-old grandchildren, grandmothers provided about seven and a half hours of child care per week; grandfathers provided five hours.

Surveys of health, aging and retirement in 10 European countries found grandparents to be very involved in their grandchildren's care across all the countries, with significant variation by gender. Among couples still in the labor force, grandfathers provided an average of about seven hours of care a week for grandchildren 12 or younger; grandmothers provided 11 hours. The amount of child care increased after retirement, to an average of 21 hours per couple, with the most significant effect on grandfathers. Employed grandfathers did 27 percent of the child care provided by grandparents and 41 percent when retired.

National surveys in the United States found that almost two-thirds of grandparents provided at least some care to grandchildren over a 10-year period, with grandmothers more likely than grandfathers to start and continue babysitting. The percentage providing child care for grandchildren declined steeply with age, from half of those in their 60s and early 70s providing care to less than one-third among grandparents ages 75-84. That study found among those in their 60s and early 70s, a larger percentage of grandfathers than grandmothers provided child care.

We asked grandparents if they currently provide care to their grandchildren or have done so in the past. The care provided varied from regularly scheduled days several times a week to at least occasional child care. We found some difference by gender: 69 percent of grandmothers and 58 percent of grandfathers provided at least occasional grandchild care. We also found that sometimes spouses did babysitting together and sometimes separately. Some grandparents described occasional variation in how each spouse handled things. One grandfather said that his wife, a former kindergarten teacher, picked up the kids after pre-school three days a week and then did things like reading and crafts while he taught them to swim and did other outdoor activities. Another grandfather told us that for their grandchildren who lived a 2½-hour drive away, "It can range from emergency babysitting (with enough advance notice due to travel time) or planned child care, if the parents have work-related activities and the normal sitter is not available. Sometimes Grandma will leave Grandpa at home for a couple of days when a longer time period is involved."

As we noted earlier, most grandparents we talked to feel very attached to their grandchildren, with virtually no difference between grandmothers and grandfathers. Some grandparents do see interaction differences, however. For example, one grandfather said his grandchildren "really like interacting with my

64

wife much more and she is much more involved with them when they are young. There isn't too much for me to do until they are about 12 or 13. Then I can do things like play sports and so on." Another grandfather told us, "I sometimes go to visit the 'far away' grandkids and their parents by myself. When my wife is there, the kids only want to be with her. Alone I have a better chance of them interacting with me." One complained that "if the grandkids come to our house, Grandma's focus is entirely on them, and nothing I say receives any attention from her!" One grandmother described her husband as less involved. "He doesn't like to crawl around on the floor. As they get older he will get more involved as he likes science. But their other grandfather [a widower] doesn't have a choice. He's it. So he's actively involved with them."

We asked grandparents to tell us their views about what grandparents should and should not do as well as what advice they would give to new grandparents. Most grandparents agreed that grandparents should "be there" but not interfere and hold back on offering opinions and advice unless specifically asked. There is a slight difference by gender. Sixteen percent of the grandfathers and 11 percent of the grandmothers said they offer unsolicited advice at least occasionally.

When we compared what grandparents said about other roles, as the table on the next page shows shows, we found both similarities and differences by gender. Grandmothers stressed loving grandchildren and helping them and their parents, whereas grandfathers emphasized teaching grandchildren values and being good role models. For example, grandmothers said things like:

"Grandparents can help to relieve the exhaustion of parenthood."

"As grandparents, we should be lovingly supportive and generous with both our grandchildren and their parents, our kids. By generous, I do not mean in the giving of money or things, but generous with our time and attention."

"Give your grandchildren as much love as you can and be there for them."

Typical of comments from grandfathers were these:

"Grandparents should play, teach, guide, set a good example, always say and demonstrate the positive and the potential all children have. They should correct in a positive manner"

"I think grandparents should be there for the grandkids as a sort of 'high-status friend' -- someone who can provide them with guidance, teaching, and maybe some teasing. Grandparents should be there for the grandkids, but not be overly intrusive."

What Grandparents Said They Should Do,
by Gender

Grandparents said that grandparents "should"	Percentage of the 156 grandmothers	Percentage of the 68 grandfathers
Love their grandchildren	57%	24%
Help their grandchildren, their children and children-in-law	55%	10%
Teach their grandchildren (including teaching values), set a good example, be a positive influence, and/or be a role model for grandchildren	19%	28%
Be emotionally supportive of the grandchildren, listen to and encourage them as they grow up	20%	19%
Just enjoy the grandchildren	20%	18%
Give financial assistance to the grandchildren and/or the household	6%	7%

Gender has an impact on the nature of the grandparent-grandchild relationship, but it is not the only factor that affects it. The ages of  the grandchildren and grandparents, the individual personalities, the behavior that each generation thinks appropriate, and the connections with the generation in between are all important in creating and maintaining inter-generational bonds. One grandmother told us with disapproval about a sister-in-law who announced to her children that when they had children she would never babysit. The sister-in-law kept her word after her grandchildren were born. The grandmother told us that as a result of her sister-in-law's decision, she stepped in. She has helped out with child care for the children of her niece and feels rewarded emotionally by connecting in this way to her grandnieces.

As we discussed in Chapter 3, the gender of the adult child is also not a primary factor. What matters more is the value placed on family held by adult children. One grandmother noted that she has a strong a relationship with her daughter-in-law, who considers family very important. Her son holds the same value -- a factor that was important in their decision to marry. The grandmother knows that her daughter-in-law hopes her sons will also value family when they become adults.

What's a Grandparent to Do?

Both grandmothers and grandfathers can be active grandparents. *Offer love, support and the benefit of your experience and interests to your grandchildren. Grandfathers and grandmothers can learn new skills if they need to.*

Grandparenting can be done together or separately. *If you feel like the less preferred grandparent, try spending time with the grandchildren on your own. That way you and the grandchildren can learn more about each other and form your own relationships.*

Respect the other grandparents. *In all likelihood, you are not the only grandparent. Be respectful of the others and do not compete. Form your own relationships with your grandchildren, so they can get to know who you are and how much you love them.*

Give your grandchildren the freedom to explore feelings and behaviors. *There will be plenty of time for your grandchildren to learn how to conform to social expectations. You can be a nonjudgmental influence by letting them try out things that their peers may not encourage. Have a tea party with your grandson, play super hero with your granddaughter, and the like. You'll both enjoy expanding their horizons.*

CHAPTER 6

The Benefits of Being an Active Grandparent

Grandparents typically do not have young children of their own and often have relatively little interaction with youngsters other than their grandchildren. This gives them both time to nurture their grandchildren and makes the intergenerational interaction valuable to them. Many grandparents told us that their role in the family enriches their lives and broadens their perspectives in a variety of ways.

For many, being a grandparent is a reprise of parenthood that enables them to see their families in new ways. One told us: "These youngsters remind me of my now-adult children as children. My children reminded me of me and my siblings when we were children. So I get the wonderful experience of revisiting both prior generations while I enjoy getting

71

to know this one. Also, I love seeing my adult children as parents." Grandparents often noted that they appreciate their grandchildren's development more than they did that of their own children because they are more experienced and less stressed by the 24/7 demands they experienced as parents. As one said, "The best thing for me about being a grandparent is that the routine home upkeep and necessary discipline are minimal, and the time for personal interaction is more available when they are around."

Another way grandparents are enriched is by grandchildren introducing them to new things. As one said, "The things they teach you!" A grandmother told us that her grandchildren helped her choose a smart phone and showed her how to use it. Another commented that she learned to use Instagram so she can view photos of the grandchildren that her daughter posts. One detailed what being a grandparent has taught her: "I have learned about weather systems from one grandchild. Another has brought back memories of the '70s with his incredible guitar expertise. A third has taught me bravery and acceptance of your true self. A fourth has taught me that a sense of humor is essential. A fifth has taught me that our differences make us unique."

Being a noncustodial grandparent is a rewarding role. Researchers conclude that the more time spent with grandchildren and the greater the range and frequency of activities, the greater the levels of life satisfaction and the more grandparents feel that they are making the world a better place by caring for others. In addition, feeling successful and competent as a grandparent and having close relationships with grandchildren is associated with better mental health.

 One particular aspect is the opportunity to be silly and spontaneous, which being with grandchildren encourages. Research indicates that adults with high levels of playfulness are better able to cope with stress and to enjoy active lifestyles. Silliness makes people laugh, which lowers blood pressure and exercises muscles. Grandparents mentioned tickling, dressing up, and making up funny songs and stories -- all aspects of silliness.

Several grandparents spoke of grandchildren helping them after a spouse died, and research supports this. Being a grandfather "helped me cope with the loss of my wife, because when they ask questions about Grandma they just want to know more about her, especially the ones that have been born since she passed away," one man said. "I hope it gives them an example of how to deal with loss." He added, "I'm a grandfather, although as a widower I try to remain aware of things that their grandmother would do if she were still alive." Even more dramatically, one woman said that "being a grandparent saved my life. My beloved husband died and soon after I was forced to retire from my job, so life was colorless. My grandson fills my heart." Such a positive outcome is not always the case, though. One grandfather noted that his contact with grandchildren diminished after his wife died, although they still keep in touch as needed.

In the United States, most grandparents have adult grandchildren, although that was not yet true of some of our participants. Although grandparents provide more expressive and instrumental support for their young grandchildren than they receive, this often changes when the grandchildren become adults. One study found that grandparents perceived their adult grandchildren provided them with more support than they received.

Some of our respondents with adult grandchildren spoke of needing and getting assistance. A few had moved into their children's home or nearby, so they could get help. One grandfather said, "I am 87 and dealing with Parkinson's. My son and my grandson (age 29) are very helpful with taking care of stuff I can't do myself. And they do it with eagerness. Psychologically they are helpful, too. We are on the same wavelength politically and enjoy talking about politics. My grandson lives closer now, so I see him more often."

Research on adult grandchildren providing care, while scarce, indicates that they generally serve as auxiliary caregivers for their grandparents and provide emotional support when their parents are primary caregivers. Adult grandchildren attempt to meet the emotional needs of their grandparents by cheering them up, talking about the past, sharing good memories, and doing their best to preserve the dignity of the grandparents. Establishing close relationships with grandchildren when they are young increases the likelihood of their company and auxiliary care when they are adults. And, of course, the generation in between matters. A national survey of adult grandchildren found that positive connections between parents and grandparents predicted positive connections between adult grandchildren and grandparents.

Development in late adulthood

Personal growth is important at all stages of life and "grandchildren clearly contribute to aging in a rich environment," as a 75-year-old grandfather put it. Another told us that "it's helped me stay active; it's helped me connect with a new generation; it's taught me the value of patience and letting children learn and explore without correction. It's helped me feel young. But honestly, sometimes it also reminds me that I'm getting older." Other comments included these:

"It is making me more politically active to help insure a better life for them."

"Keeps us mentally and physically occupied with numerous events, sports, and activities."

"It has been a great source of love and of being in a position to love. It has made me more future-oriented (from short-term like planning our visits to the longest views of where the grandkids are going in their lives) and at the same time more firmly 'in the moment' when we are with them."

The consensus was that grand-parenting keeps the mind younger. Grandparenting as a key factor in health and cognitive preservation as one ages is supported by research.

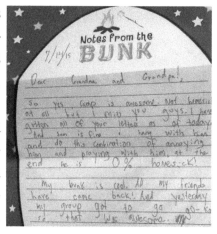

Being a grandparent is not essential to enjoying one's later years and coming to terms with the limits of life, but according to almost all of our grandparents, it adds new experiences and reminds of earlier ones. Psychological theorists consider it desirable for aging adults to expand personal interests and develop concern for the next generation. This can take the form of nurturing, mentoring, teaching, and promoting the welfare of those who will follow.

While parenting and many professions provide such opportunities, when children leave home and retirement nears, grandparenting adds a special opportunity to further nurture adult children, as well as the new generation. Long-term studies of women and men have found that successful aging is related to deepening commitment to the welfare of their families and those they mentor. For both women and men, reviewing one's earlier years as child and parent contributes to the life review process that is part of satisfaction in the later years.

Despite the challenge of not being in control, our grandparents said they enjoy the special position of providing love, attention and assistance without the full responsibility they had as parents. The slogan "Attention, Availability, Acceptance" coined by one grandmother reflects the special focus of grandparents in contrast to parents. Telling family stories, teaching family traditions, and learning new ways of relating to adult children and a new generation can support integrity in the last developmental stage of late adulthood. For many people, involvement with grandchildren contributes to living a meaningful life.

Benefits for Families

While two-thirds of Italian grandparents and slightly more than half of German grandparents believe they have a responsibility to help with child care for their grandchildren, only one-third of American grandparents hold this view. Despite it not being a "should" for most Americans, many noncustodial grandparents are actively involved in the care of their grandchildren.

In Chapter 4, we discussed the ways in which grandparents are particularly helpful to parents with special-needs grandchildren. We found grandparents of typically developing children actively involved as well. Two-thirds of the grandparents we talked to said they had provided at least some child care. Sometimes the child care is regularly scheduled, but often grandparents are called upon at the last minute, such as when illness, school closings or an emergency disrupts the normal routine. The grandparent who helps out helps all three generations: grandchildren,

 adult children and grandparents. The impact of grandparent involvement on children and adults has been most often studied when children are in need of preschool care. Researchers have found that involvement by a grandmother is a protective factor for at-risk children. Grandparents can protect children from harsh parenting and increase the social competence of preschool children. Children ages 11 to 16 typically value grandparent involvement and feel they benefit from it. The positive impact of financial and emotional involvement of grandparents continues through the school years, the teen years and into adulthood.

Being engaged and active is a goal for many grandparents. Our next chapters discuss some ways to achieve that by building and maintaining intergenerational bonds.

What's a Grandparent to Do?

Enjoy reminiscing. Watching a new generation is a good reminder of earlier stages of your life. Enjoy the process; it is a healthy aspect of the mature years.

Teach what you know. As a trusted member of the family, you can introduce the grandchildren to your interests and expertise. Do you like puzzles, fishing, baking, building models? Sharing activities with the grandchildren enriches the experience for everyone. Having more than one grandchild participate enables them to know each other better.

Learn from them. Grandchildren can teach you about the books they read, the music they enjoy, and the many electronic skills and games they master. Broaden your horizons by watching, asking and learning.

Establish the basis for continuing connection. The more you share time and interests when they are young, the more likely that your relationship will be meaningful when they become adults and you are elderly.

80

Realize that your connection to the grandchildren benefits all three generations. *The attention and care you provide the grandchildren assists them and their parents, as well as enriching your days.*

CHAPTER 7

How to be an Engaged Grandparent

Noncustodial grandparents get time off as well as time on, in contrast to parents who are on 24/7. One grandmother told us: "I feel enormous love for the grandkids, and it's not impacted by such confounders like the shoulds, musts, schedules, exhaustion and financial constraints that I felt as a parent. I have much more patience and maybe even desire to 'play' at a kid's level. And the 'playing' certainly adds a form of relaxation that I hadn't quite discovered when I had kids of my own. I now am able to grow down and slow down; this experience has been an eye-opener in terms of understanding myself and what made and makes me tick." Indeed, grandmothers do considerably less multitasking than mothers. Grandfathers and fathers typically do the same amount of multitasking as they are likely to read the paper or check email while doing child care.

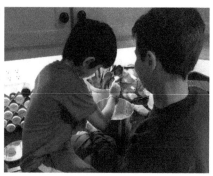

Active grandparents are in the moment, or mindful, when with their grandchildren. Mindfulness refers to being actively aware and engaged with the environment. Research indicates that children perceive mindfulness on the part of those who care for them and that it has positive effects on them, when compared to being in the care of adults who are mentally distracted and only pretending interest in the children's conversation or activity.

Active grandparenting of babies and young children requires being hands-on. As one grandmother said, "I love the intimacy of being with grandchildren. They are so physical, immediate and trusting. When I am with them, they make me stay in the moment. I focus on their interests and needs when they are young. I add sharing my interests as they get older. All of my grandkids think I love games and puzzles. I do, but they would be surprised how little of that I do when I am not with them." Getting on the floor with little ones or taking them on one's lap to read or chat facilitates active engagement. As grandchildren get older, engaged grandparents ask informed questions and share their own interests in puzzles, games, sports, music, museums, science, etc. Learning about teenage grandchildren's interests and activities can help to maintain connection at a time when the teenagers are spending more time away from the family.

Time together

As with most relationships, those between grandparents and grandchildren depend primarily on the quality of time spent together (in person or electronically). Many of our grandparents indicated this in one way or another. One grandmother had this advice: "Go to see the kids in their own home. Kids profit from it and you profit from it. Kids are different when they are at home than when they are in other places. Get as involved as you can. Play games, read a book, do a puzzle, get on the floor, take them to the supermarket." Another offered, "Have something which sets you apart -- some activity, story, book you can share over phone or using social media." One grandmother said she is asked to read the same book, "Good Queen Bess," every time her granddaughter visits because they both love it so much. Another reads and rereads poetry from a favorite collection.

Grandparents utilize a variety of strategies to connect with their grandchildren. A grandfather told of bringing his guitar to his granddaughter's preschool, at her request, to sing with her friends. One grandmother described her visits to her grandchildren's classrooms. "When each was in day care, I would pick up him or her when I visited, so I could see the space and meet the teachers. As they began to walk and talk, I would go early for pick-up and spend time playing with the children or participating in the planned activity, so I could know their friends. When they were in preschool, I would offer to do a project. One easy and successful one was about cats. I brought a book about cats to read and cat-shaped cookies I had baked, which the children then decorated. I visited grammar school classes as well, volunteering to help or observe, as best suited the teacher's plan for the day. My grandchildren love having me in their class, the parents love hearing about my observations, and I love feeling more connected to their daily routines."

Another grandmother told us, "Enjoy the fun of being a grandparent. Save some money so when they are a little older you can really do something great. I spent way too much money on baby stuff or toys that never lasted or things I wanted them to have that they really did not care about. (For example when I travelled they didn't always like the tee shirt or the Swedish doll I thought was lovely.) So don't waste money . . . save for the experiences you can provide."

Said another grandmother: "The advice I would give a new grandparent is to see their grandchildren as much and as often while they are young. Let the parents have their own space while you visit. I think you bond with the children when their parents are not around. I think sleepovers really help solidify the relationship. I think finding something unique about each grandchild makes them each feel special." Similarly, a grandfather of seven said, "As the grandchildren get older the relationship evolves and the interactions with each child take on the flavor of each child's personality. From my perspective that's better because then each relationship is special in its own way." One grandmother found that the middle grandchild in one household is quieter than the others and in a group does not often speak his mind, but during special one-on-one time he is talkative.

A grandmother with an interest in bird-watching and identification developed a gifting strategy to engage her grandchildren. "One year the presents for all the grandchildren were all about birds: a bird feeder with seeds, Bird Bingo, a few Audubon Singing Birds with real bird calls recorded inside that played when squeezed, jigsaw puzzles with bird motifs and a bird-house that we attached to a tree they could see from their kitchen window. They all reported periodically on the birds they'd seen, with the cat being the most appreciative viewer as she watched from inside the window."

A grandfather said he loves sharing old cartoons and television shows with his grandchildren. "When they come to my house, they ask to see "old" Super-man and the comedy routines of Laurel and Hardy" he told us. They remind him of his youth and intro-duce the youngsters to how things used to be.

Help out with permission

Parents are often overwhelmed. Grandparents may offer to help in ways that their children would appreciate. Grandparents can do things like babysit for grandchildren, bring food for the family (and

stock the freezer with pre-cooked meals as well), do laundry, become the extra adult at special events such as birthday parties, drive grandchildren to activities and appointments. Some grandparents offer to pay for "extras" like a week at camp or sports equipment that would strain the family budget. Others are the family photographers, recording the children's growth and adventures and presenting the families with albums or photobooks. Offer help that you can afford in terms of time and money, but try not to be insulted if the offers are sometimes rebuffed.

Changes over time

As grandchildren grow and develop, grandparents must be prepared for changes in skill level, interests and activities. Unlike parents, grandparents do not typically see the changes day-to-day and have to catch up from visit to visit. One grandmother described two grandsons "totally involved in Pokémon Go." They insisted that she put the app on her phone and then "go to parks and other venues so they could catch new Pokémon and battle in the gyms (and yes, I had to learn the lingo). They would ask about my new Pokémon every time I talked to them." But after six months "their love affair with this game was over and I had to find new interests in order to connect with them."

Such changes provide opportunities for grandparents to introduce new activities. One grandmother said she likes to do puzzles and play games. As her grandchildren have developed skills, she has been able to introduce more difficult puzzles and teach them new games. She also has learned games from them. Another grandmother, with five grandsons said simply, "Boys -- video games!"

Grandchildren sometimes develop new food preferences and dislikes. Grandmothers told of buying all the old favorites before a visit and having them go uneaten. Grandmothers also spoke of needing to stay attuned to parental "rules" about food. "Different styles in different houses," one explained. "One daughter and her husband are into healthy eating. Another daughter is just learning to cook; her kids snack all the time. Different styles, but I have no conflict." Some grandparents told us that when with grandchildren, they use "grandparent rules," which is fine as long as parents are aware of this strategy. For example, one told of not allowing soda when she is providing the meals, whether at home or out to eat. When the parents are present, their rules prevail.

Special events

A frequently mentioned way of connecting is by sharing trips. We discuss this more fully in Chapter 8, because it is especially important for grandparents who have some or all of their grandchildren living at a distance. Grandparents also frequently mentioned sharing holidays and other special occasions as a way of connecting the generations. After infancy, grandchildren remember the routines and rituals, and pictures of themselves as babies at these events delight them. Traditions can be passed on from earlier generations, created fresh, or old and new combined. At only four years old, one granddaughter reminded her grandmother that she was going to help make the pumpkin pie for Thanksgiving.

Special concerns

Several grandparents warned of potential pitfalls in well-meaning actions. One was: Do not compare grandchildren, whether siblings or cousins. They each have their own strengths and weaknesses, and they each need to feel love and respect for who they are. Another was: Keep an eye to equitable treatment of different adult children's households. This is complicated when some are near and some are far, some are welcoming and some less so, or some are easy to get along with and others more difficult. No hard-and-fast rule exists, but keeping attuned to fairness and being open about choices can help. One grandmother spoke about her grandchildren being different ages in different households, so she cannot do the same trips with all of the kids. Her strategy is to be honest about what she is doing with the older ones, and promising an age-appropriate alternative for the younger ones.

Take care of yourself

Whatever the level of engagement, grandparents must make sure they do not deprive themselves by not doing things they want  to do in order to meet the needs of children and grandchildren. When grandparents give up too much, dissatisfaction can spill over into family relationships. If there is something that is important to you, invite grandchildren to join you or ask for "time off." Without the sense that grandparent-grandchild time is a choice, you might feel resentment, which is not useful for anyone.

Make sensible "grandparent rules" to help things work. For example, one grandmother put a digital clock where grandchildren sleeping over could see it and established the rule that everyone stays in bed and does not wake others before 7:00 AM. This is especially helpful when time zones have been crossed. Caring for tired and cranky children is not fun. Likewise, being cared for by tired and cranky grandparents is not fun either.

Planning a few days for recovery after time with grandchildren is a good idea. Many grandparents have colds after a visit with the grandchildren. During a visit, "Take deep breaths, exercise, prepare to be near bacteria," advised a grandmother. "Getting sick from all their germs. We are past that stage now, because they are older, but after visits we would be sick for two or three weeks."

Others talked about exhaustion. As one grandmother put it, "Looking after grandchildren is tiring -- we don't have the same energy that we had when we were younger." Another said, "Sometimes grandchildren can make you feel very young and sometimes they can make you feel very old." One acknowledged no longer having "the energy of a 20-year-old." By way of example, another said, "We recently took them on a day trip. Overall it was fun, but an exhausting eight hours!" A few mentioned planning ahead. "We planned out the visits to be fresh and energetic. This made everything work out well when they were here."

When asked what the worst thing about being a grandparent was, some mentioned energy level. Said a grandfather, "The worst thing is always having to maintain the level of energy required to keep up with them." A 62-year-old woman who described herself as "a physically active grandma" acknowledged that "as we get older we lose our patience a little quicker. As my mom always said, 'That's why God gives you children when you're young.' So I guess the worst thing can tie into this."

What's a Grandparent to Do?

Stay in the moment. *Try to put aside your worries and focus on the activities of the moment. Even when you need a break, you can be engaged with the grandchildren by watching and talking.*

Spend time alone with each grandchild. *When possible, give the parents a break and yourself the treat of one-on-one time with each child. Doing age-appropriate activities with each child individually will help you get to know each other better.*

Do not take changes in grandchildren's interests and preferences personally. *Children* *change their minds about what they like to eat and play, sometimes daily and certainly as they grow older. Be flexible and open-minded, so you can appreciate each stage.*

Develop "grandparent rules" for when you are in charge. *You cannot make the general rules, but when you are alone with them you can make provisional rules. For example, some grandparents add sweet treats; others limit them. Some enforce "indoor voices"; others do not. Be yourself, but do not contradict major parental rules.*

Do not compare and contrast siblings or cousins. *Grandchildren each have strengths and weaknesses. Nurture the former; help them overcome the latter. Do not judge or compare grandchildren, or your children and grandchildren may become defensive.*

Keep equity in mind as you interact with different households. *Some families may live closer than others or may be more welcoming. Grandchildren will be at different ages and have different needs. Remember that equal treatment*

95

may not be possible, but keep equity in mind in your interactions.

Take care of yourself. *Your health and well-being are important. Be sure to build in recovery time after exposure to germs and exhausting activities.*

CHAPTER 8

Long-Distance Active Grandparenting

G randparents who live near grandchildren can sometimes be spontaneous and visit on a moment's notice. Long-distance grandparents -- living anywhere from 90 to several thousand miles away from grandchildren – do not have that option. While distance adds one more variable, we found that it is not insurmountable. What follows are some suggestions for connecting across the miles.

Visit grandchildren often

If you are fortunate enough to have the financial resources and time to visit grandchildren frequently, do so, especially when grandchildren are young. In the early years, before friends, school and activities

97

make life more complicated, grandparents are likely to be welcome visitors.

Talking to the parents well in advance will help in planning visits for times that are mutually convenient. As the schedules of children and grandchildren are likely to be more crowded than yours, it is useful to be as flexible as possible.

It is always nice to find special events in your grandchildren's geographic area to which you might be able to treat the kids or perhaps the whole family. Is there a fair, a children's theater performance, a sporting event or something else you think they would enjoy? Check with the parents and then make plans for the special activity during your visit.

If you have a skill or interest that you want to share, visits are a perfect time to do so. One grandfather brought the fishing pole that his grandfather had made for him and took the grandchildren fishing each summer visit. Another who loved going to farms and farm stands researched what was being picked at local orchards and farms and took the grandchildren berry and apple picking. One grandmother reported that special foods are available at her local markets, so before each visit she asks grandchildren for their requests.

Taking kids to age-appropriate movies can be fun. Or get the DVD or streaming version to view with them. You will get the opportunity to see some good movies and to hear your grandchildren's opinions about them. Our next chapter includes websites with recommendations for movies for different ages.

Remember that you are on your grandchildren's home turf, so fit into their activities and schedules whenever possible. Be sure to watch soccer games, ballet recitals, swimming lessons and the like. And don't be insulted if your grandchildren choose being with friends instead of you some of the time. You will find you can learn a great deal about grandchildren's lives, friends and interests over a weekend.

Be respectful of the household style. As one grandmother told us, "When visiting, 'grands' should recognize the level of household order their adult children prefer and work to maintain that. 'Grands' should not try to make improvements or reorganize." Although some adult children welcome help or even suggest household projects they think suit their parents' talents and their households' needs, others prefer that grandparents keep "hands off" and interpret suggestions as criticism.

If they visit you, make it easy and fun

If your children and grandchildren are willing and able to visit you, be grateful. Clear your schedule and make it a fun and welcoming visit. Think about

99

making your home as hospitable as possible -- perhaps putting special things in the rooms where they sleep and hang out to make them feel at home. Cook family favorites and invite children into the kitchen to help or learn.

If there are activities in your area that would be appropriate for children of their ages, be sure to offer these as options. For example, libraries or bookstores may offer story hours, many towns have interesting playgrounds, and libraries may have community memberships to local venues such as museums and zoos that you can reserve.

A few grandmothers told us about "grandma camp" for one or more weeks during summer vacation. Sometimes the kids slept over and sometimes it was day camp. In either case, the grandparent made plans for each day -- time at a zoo, a library, a museum, a ball game, etc. One grandmother reported that she did this for several summers and the grandchildren reported that they liked "grandma camp" much better than their regular summer camp.

Have a special box of "grandparent stuff"

While giving gifts to grandchildren is one of the special joys of being a grandparent, keep some things in reserve that are only available when you

visit them or they visit you. Your things -- and by association, you -- are special and part of your visits. There are easily transportable items to keep in this box, such as a deck of cards, stickers, crafts materials, a favorite book, a game for two or more players, a set of storytelling cards, small puppets and the like. Playing a game or reading a book a few times a year makes it something that a grandchild can look forward to without being bored by its constant presence.

Initiate communication frequently

Grandparents told us about the variety of ways they keep in touch with grandchildren, such as sending cards, letters and small gifts. Because children rarely get personal mail any more, grandchildren look forward these special deliveries. If you want to receive mail from them, make it easy. You can buy postcards, stamp them and address them to yourself. One grandfather created a short questionnaire for grandchildren to fill out and mail back to him with questions like "What's the weather like there?" and "What was your favorite activity at school today?"

One grandmother told us that although she had little interest before, once her grandsons got old enough to be sports fans, she learned about their favorite teams. Not only did she send team memorabilia as birthday gifts, but she tried to watch at least part of most games, find out the final scores and send texts after the game with her comments. She said her grandsons loved that they could connect with her about many things, including the sports and teams they followed.

Use technology to keep connected

A computer, tablet, or smart phone will be useful for keeping in touch across the miles. Recruit one of the parents to be your "liaison" with the child because without parental encouragement and enthusiasm, this method of connecting is not likely to happen. If the parents are willing, FaceTime or Skype can enable periodic "visits." Even babies soon learn to recognize their grandparents' faces and voices. Young children like to listen to grandparents talk to them, show them picture books, sing songs with them or watch a short grandparent puppet show. Older children can tell about their activities, and grandparents can share information about their own adventures. One grandfather described sending gifts for his grand-daughters ahead of  time so his daughter could organize birthday "visits" for grandpa to see his granddaughters open them in front of the computer.

Older children can connect with grandparents on social media platforms -- of course using proper "etiquette." Texting with older children and, if they are willing, having email communication with them can be a useful way to have short interactions.

Phones still work and it is nice to hear each other's voices. Short conversations may work best and can be useful for when the child is in the car. One grandfather would call on the parent's mobile phone and ask the child to describe what she saw out the window as she was being driven to preschool.

Apps for your devices are constantly being developed, so check out lists on websites that review them. One such site, Common Sense Media (https://www.commonsensemedia.org), is an independent nonprofit organization that aims to provide information and advice about media and technology in children's lives. An example of a highly rated app

103

is ustyme, a video chat program much like Skype, that has a library of ebooks and games that can be used for shared reading and play. Other apps, such as Words With Friends, a Scrabble-style game played with remote opponents, can be used once children can read and spell. Apps that include a chat feature, as does Words With Friends, add to the appeal and help to stay in touch.

Travel and vacation together

Many long-distance grandparents told about the special experience of family vacations with their children and grandchildren. Gatherings at summer homes or rentals with all members of the family can enhance extended family connections. One grandfather told of the great fun he had taking four of his grandchildren on weekend trips to nearby cities. A grandmother described her vacations at the beach. "It is a fantastic time. We spend lots of time at the beach, walks, sharing meals. We have early dinner, then babysit, so parents can have time to themselves. Win, win!" Another grandmother said, "We used to take weeklong vacations together at least once a year, which were always joyous and interesting, Yellowstone, Galapagos, Costa Rica, Sedona. . . . It is getting more difficult to find a time that all nine of us are available at the same time, but I have just booked a trip to Iceland for June -- keeping my fingers crossed that it will happen for all of us."

Other grandparents reported taking trips with grandchildren without their parents or siblings. For some grandparents, the magic age was 10; for others it was 12. In each case, the grandparent invited input from the grandchild about where they would like to go. We heard about the lucky grandchild who got her wish of attending a one-week drama program in London with her grandparents; another told about visiting several Italian cities during a school vacation. One grandparent told of taking age-mate cousins on special trips. Other grandparents took advantage of already organized trips, such as the intergenerational experiences by Road Scholar.

Some grandparents spend considerable amounts of money on their grandchildren, often for gifts and sometimes for necessities. In contrast, from some we heard of wishes for trips to Disney World that were

105

too expensive to take. We also heard of families in which successful adult children rented a vacation house or invited grandparents to join them for a family vacation. For some, there were enjoyable local but special outings with grandchildren -- to parks, museums, pools, playgrounds or beaches -- requiring little or no money. Whether distant or local, trips provide opportunities for informal learning and bonding.

Ways of organizing this type of experience and of planning multi-generational trips should be discussed so that no one absorbs all the financial cost or all of the work. One pattern our respondents described was to have all the adults take turns planning, shopping for and preparing meals. Once "house rules" are set, spending multiple days and nights together can be a terrific way for adult children to get to know nieces and nephews, for cousins to connect, and for grandparents to enjoy all the children and grandchildren.

Ways to celebrate your time together

Make memories about your shared time together and save them in some way. Teach children to take photographs, encourage them to think of things to put in an album or memory box, help them write journal entries about the visit, trip or vacation.

Working together to create journals, photo books or videos of their time spent with you can be a wonderful activity with lasting benefits.

Children like to remember favorite times. One grandmother shared a story from a holiday visit with her family. She said the older grandchildren pulled out photo books from trips taken with the grandparents and paged through them with great interest. After they all shared their memories, they told her how much they were anticipating the next trip.

On trips or vacations, grandparents can "debrief" the grandchildren at the end of the day, asking them what they most liked about it and perhaps taking notes or starting a journal for them. Grandparents also can lend or give a camera to a grandchild or have discussions about what to include in a photo book or video. Once the grandchildren become engaged in the process, they might point out things to photograph or suggest posing for photos for you to take.

One grandmother made a few photo books for her grandchildren based on her visits to them and from trips taken together. She found that the oldest liked them so much he wanted to become her co-author. She agreed, and he soon provided suggestions for the next books they created, including "Friends and Family," "Work and Play" and "Treasures and Adventures."

Be creative and take risks. If one method does not work, try others. Building bonds takes time and energy. The results are worth it.

CHAPTER 9

Resources for Grandparents

S earch the web, ask your friends or go to the library. You will find an enormous amount of information about how to grandparent, as well as suggestions for activities and adventures. Here are some resources to consider.

1. Organizations and websites for grandparents

- The National Association for Grandparenting was founded in 2016 to help grandparents by discussing best practices, research and information for grandparents of grandchildren of all ages. With the motto "connecting hearts, uniting generations," the organization offers

a free weekly emailed newsletter. http://
www.grandsmatter.org

- The American Grandparents Association
  offers advice and services on grandparenting
  and other issues (such as health, well-being,
  Medicare). The site says it has almost 2 million members and offers free information on
  its site as well as a paid subscription option.
  For example, one free article offers a list of
  100 free things to do with your grandchildren.
  https://aga.grandparents.com/

- AARP has hundreds of articles about and advice for grandparents on it site for Americans
  over 50. For example, see https://www.aarp.
  org/home-family/friends-family/info-2016/
  how-to-grandparent-fairly-mq.html   and
  https://travel.aarp.org/articles-tips/articles/
  info-07-2013/family-vacation-ideas.html

- Grand Magazine for Grandparents bills itself
  as "the lifestyle magazine for AWESOME
  grandparents." Its website includes many
  articles on grandparenting, including activities to do with grandchildren. https://www.
  grandparentslink.com/

2. Grandparent/grandchild travel

Quite a few companies have trips for grandparents and grandchildren, including the following:

- Road Scholar has several hundred multi-generational trips available both within the United States and internationally. The organization notes that the focus is "educational and fun" and includes field trips, performances and lectures. https://www.roadscholar.org/travel-resources/grandparents/

- Smithsonian Journeys offers family adventure tours with a variety of activity levels, interests and locals. https://www.smithsonianjourneys.org/

- Journeys International offers a wide variety of international family trips. Its site specifies that the trips are for those "six to seventy six." https://www.journeysinternational.com/journeys-families/multi

- Tauck Tours offers a variety of family-oriented group experiences both locally and abroad.

111

http://www.tauck.com/family-travel/why-tauck-bridges/multi-generational-travel.aspx

- A website that focuses on family travel, including grandparents, and covers issues such as cruises, travel insurance and traveling with teens, is https://myfamilytravels.com/

3. Video, technology and toy recommendations

- Common Sense is a leading independent, nonprofit organization focused on media and technology for children. Check out its lists of apps, games, books, movies, TV shows and websites. Receiving no payment for the reviews, the site offers media ratings based on age appropriateness and learning potential. https://www.commonsensemedia.org/

- Parents' Choice Foundation is a nonprofit that offers guides to children's media and toys. The site includes awards for audio, magazines, toys, books, video games, DVDs, apps and software. Best known for the Parents' Choice Awards® program, the Parents' Choice Award Seals

112

are selected by a team of judges. http://www.
parents-choice.org/allawards.cfm

- The British Academy of Film and Television Arts (BAFTA) is an independent arts charity that gives awards in a variety of categories including films, television and video games for children. http://www.bafta.org/children

- *Parents Magazine* has a listing of the 50 best videos for children. https://www.parents.com/fun/entertainment/movies/50-best-videos-for-kids/

- Magazines, including *Good Housekeeping* and *Parents Magazine*, give annual awards for children's toys.

- The website Modern Parents Messy Kids lists what it calls "brain-growing, and yet still super-fun toys" that are arranged into themed guides and categorized by recommended age ranges. https://modernparentsmessykids.com/2017-top-toy-awards/

- The independent consumer organization, Oppenheim Toy Portfolio, gives annual awards for the most outstanding toys each year. https://www.prnewswire.com/news/ oppenheim-toy-portfolio

4. Award winning books

- The Newbery Medal is awarded annually by the American Library Association to the author of the most distinguished contribution to American literature for children. http://www.ala.org/alsc/awardsgrants/ bookmedia/newberymedal/newberymedal

- The Caldecott Medal is awarded annually by a division of the American Library Association to the artist of the most distinguished American picture book for children. http://www. ala.org/alsc/awardsgrants/bookmedia/ caldecottmedal/caldecottmedal

- The Coretta Scott King Book Awards are given annually to outstanding African American authors and illustrators of books for children and young adults that demonstrate an appreciation of African American culture and universal human values. http://olos.ala.org/csk/

114

- The Pura Belpré Award is given each year to a Latino/Latina writer and illustrator whose work best portrays, affirms, and celebrates the Latino cultural experience in an outstanding work of literature for children and youth. http://www.ala.org/alsc/awardsgrants/bookmedia/belpremedal

- The Batchelder Award is given to the outstanding children's book originally published in a language other than English in a country other than the United States, and subsequently translated into English for publication in the United States. http://www.ala.org/alsc/awardsgrants/bookmedia/batchelderaward

- The Theodor Seuss Geisel Award is given annually to the author(s) and illustrator(s) of the most distinguished American book for beginning readers published in English in the United States. http://www.ala.org/alsc/awardsgrants/bookmedia/geiselaward

- The YALSA Award for Excellence in Nonfiction is given annually to the best nonfiction book published for young adults (ages 12-18) http://www.ala.org/yalsa/nonfiction.

115

- Rainbow Book List is a bibliography high-lighting books aimed at children and youth from birth to age 18 with significant gay, lesbian, bisexual, transgender, or queer/questioning content. http://glbtrt.ala.org/rainbowbooks/

- The Sydney Taylor Book Award is presented annually to outstanding books for children and teens that authentically portray the Jewish experience. http://jewishlibraries.org/Sydney_Taylor_Book_Award

- The Schneider Family Book Awards honor an author or illustrator for a book that embodies an artistic expression of the disability experience for child and adolescent audiences. http://www.ala.org/awardsgrants/schneider-family-book-award

- The Jane Addams Children's Book Award annually recognizes excellent children's books that effectively engage children in thinking about peace, social justice, global community, and equity for all people. http://www.janeaddamspeace.org/jacba/

Introduction

"Many grandparents enthusiastically responded . . ." Condon, J., Cordindale, C., Luszca, M., & Gamble, E. (2012). The Australian first time grandparents study: Time spent with the grandchild and its predictors. *Australian Journal of Aging, 32*, 21-27.

Chapter 1: Grandparents Today

"More than 70 million grandparents. . ." Krogstad, J.M. (2015). Retrieved from http://www.pewresearch.org/fact-tank/2015/09/13/5-facts-about-american-grandparents/; Grandparenting Plus (2013). Retrieved from https://www.grandparentsplus.org.uk/wp-content/uploads/2013/03/EU-report-summary.pdf; US Census. (2014). 10 percent of grandparents live with a grandchild. *Census Bureau Reports*. Retrieved from https://www.census.gov/newsroom/press-releases/2014/cb14-194.html

"Families used to be larger. . ." Widmer, E. (2010). *Family configurations: A structural approach to family diversity.* Burlington, Vt.: Ashgate Publishing.

"The timing of becoming a grandparent. . ." Burton L.M. (1996). Age norms, the timing of family role transitions, and intergenerational caregiving among aging African American women. The Gerontologist, 36, (2), 199-208; Krogstad (2015); Grandparents.com (2013). Surprising facts about grandparents. Retrieved from http://www. grandparents.com/food-and-leisure/did-you-know/ surprising-facts-about-grandparents

"Becoming a grandparent is a source of happiness. . ." Grandparents.com (2013); Livingston, G., & Parker, K. (2010). Since the start of the great recession, more children raised by grandparents retrieved from http://www. pewsocialtrends.org/2010/09/09/since-the-start-of-the-great-recession-more-children-raised-by-grandparents/

"Geographic mobility has a major influence. . ." The Met Life Report on American Grandparents. Retrieved from https://www.metlife.com/assets/cao/mmi/publications/studies/2011/mmi-american-grandparents.pdf

"Grandparents living apart from grandchildren. . ." Laughlin, L. (2013). Who's minding the kids? Child care arrangements: Spring 2011. *Current Population Reports*, 70-135. Washington, D. C.: US Census Bureau; Luo, Y, Lapierre, T.A., Hughes, M.E, & Waite, L.J. (2012). Grandparents providing care to grandchildren A population-based study of continuity and change. *Journal of Family Issues 33*(9), 1143-1167; Krogstad (2015); Statham, J. (2011). Grandparents providing child care. UK Childhood Wellbeing Research Center. Retrieved from https://www.gov.uk/government/uploads/system/uploads/attachment_data/file/181364/CWRC-00083-2011.pdf

"Grandparent age has an impact on the provision of child care. . ." Livingston & Parker (2010).

Chapter 2: Variations in the Grandparenting Experience

"Distance matters when it comes. . ." Uhlenberg, P., & Hammill, B.G. (1998). Frequency of grandparent contact with grandchild sets: Six factors that make a difference. *The Gerontologist, 38* (3): 276-285; NACCRR (National Association of Child Care Resource & Referral Agencies). (2008). Grandparents: A critical child care safety net. Retrieved from http://usa.childcareaware.org/wp-content/uploads/2015/10/2008_grandparents_report-finalrept.pdf

"Step-grandchildren/grandparent relationships are diverse." Chapman, A, Coleman, M., & Ganong, L. (2016). "Like my grandparent, but not": A qualitative investigation of skip-generation stepgrandchild-stepgrandparent relationships. *Journal of Marriage and the Family, 78,* 634-643.

"Although virtually all of the grandparents we talked to described their experiences in highly positive ways. . ." Lee, M., & Gardener, J.E. (2010). Grandparents' involvement and support in families with children with disabilities. *Educational Gerontology, 36,* 467–499; Hillman, J.L., Wentzel, M.C., & C.M. Anderson, C.M. (2017). Grandparents' experience of autism spectrum disorder: Identifying primary themes and needs. *Journal of Autism Developmental Disorders, 47,* 2957–2968.

"Another said, "I try not to give advice . . ." Tomlin, A. M. (1998). Grandparents' influences on grandchildren. In M. E. Szinovacz (Ed)., *Handbook on grandparenthood* (pp. 159-170). Westport, CT: Greenwood Press.

Chapter 3: Generation in Between

"Parents, especially new parents, have strong preferences..." Rethinking family life: Exploring the role of grandparents and the wider family. (2009). Retrieved from https://www.grandparentsplus.org.uk/rethinking-family-life; Dun, T. (2010). Turning points in parent-grandparent relationships during the start of a new generation. *Journal of Family Communication 10*(3), 194-210.

"Differing expectations regarding the grandparent role. . ." Breheny, M., Stephens, C., & Spilsbury, L. (2013). Involvement without interference: How grandparents negotiate intergenerational expectations in relationships with grandchildren. *Journal of Family Studies, 19*(2), 174-184.

"Just 10 of the grandparents we talked. . ." Fingerman, K. (2004). The role of offspring and in-laws in grandparents' ties to their grandchildren. *Journal of Family Issues 25*(8), 1026-1049.

"Even if there are complaints. . ." Fingerman (2004).

Chapter 4: Grandchildren Growing and Changing

"Other grandparents made no judgment. . ." Attar-Schwartz, S. (2015). Emotional closeness to parents and grandparents: A moderated mediation model predicting adolescent adjustment. *American Journal of Orthopsyciatry, 85,* 495-503.

"Indirect influence can take the form of giving advice . . ." Tomlin, A. M. (1998). Grandparents' influences on grandchildren. In M. E. Szinovacz (Ed.), *Handbook on grandparenthood* (pp. 159-170). Westport, CT: Greenwood Press.

"A grandfather whose grandson. . ." Griggs, J., Tan, J-P, Buchanan, A, Attar-Schwartz, S., & Flouri, E. (2010). 'They've always been there for me': Grandparental involvement and child well-being. *Children & Society, 24*, 200-214.

Chapter 5: Does Gender Matter?

"Studies of grandfathers are rare . . ." Roberto, K. A., Allen, K. R., & Blieszner, R. (2001). Grandfathers' perceptions and expectations of relationships with their adult grandchildren. *Journal of Family Issues, 22*(4), 407-426; Condon, J., Corkindale, C., Luszcz M, & Gamble, E. (2013). The Australian first-time grandparents study: Time spent with the grandchild and its predictors. *Australian Journal of Ageing 32*(1), 21-27.

"Surveys of health, aging and retirement in 10 European countries . . ." Leopold, T., & Skopek, J. (2014). Gender and the division of labor in older couples: How European grandparents share market work and childcare. *Social Forces, 93(1)*, 63–91.

"National surveys in the United States . . ." Luo et al, (2012); Livingston & Parker (2010).

"As we discussed in Chapter 3 . . ." Span, P. (2018, March 27). The maternal grandparent edge. *The New York Times*, p. D5.

Chapter 6: The Benefits of Being an Active Grandparent

"Being a noncustodial grandparent is a rewarding role." Goodman (2012); Moore, S. M. & Rosenthal, D.A. (2015). Personal growth, grandmother engagement and satisfaction among non-custodial grandmothers. *Aging & Mental Health, 19*, 2, 136-143; Reitzes D. C. Mutran E. J. (2004). Grandparent identity, intergenerational family identity, and well-being. *The Journal of Gerontology, Series B: Psychological Sciences and Social Sciences, 59*, S213– S21.

"One particular aspect is the opportunity to be silly..." Proyer, R.T. (2012). Examining playfulness in adults: Testing its correlates with personality, positive psychological functioning, goal aspirations, and multi-methodically assessed ingenuity. *Psychological Test and Assessment Modeling, 54,* 103-127.

"Several grandparents spoke of grandchildren helping them . . ." Villar, F., Celdrán, M., & Triadó C. (2012). Grandmothers offering regular auxiliary care for their grandchildren: An expression of generativity in later life? *Journal of Women & Aging, 24*(4), 292-312.

"In the United States, most grandparents have adult grandchildren. . ." Langer, N. (1990). Grandparents and adult grandchildren: What do they do for one another? *The International Journal of Aging & Human Development, 31*(2), 101-110.

"Research on adult grandchildren providing care . . ." Blanton, P.W. (2013). Family caregiving to frail elders: Experiences of young adult grandchildren as auxiliary caregivers. *Journal of Intergenerational Relationships, 11*, 1, 18-31; Piercy, K. W., & Chapman, J. G. (2001). Adopting the caregiver role: A family legacy. *Family Relations: An Interdisciplinary Journal of Applied Family Studies, 50*(4), 386-393; Hodgson, L. G. (1998). Grandparents and older grandchildren. In Ed. M.E. Szinovacz (Ed.), *Handbook on grandparenthood* (pp. 171-183). Westport, CT: Greenwood Press.

"Personal growth is important at all stages of life. . ." Burn, K., & Szoeke, C. (2015). Is grandparenting a form of social engagement that benefits cognition in ageing? *Maturitas*, *80*, 122-125.

"Being a grandparent is not essential . . ." Erikson, E. (1980). *Identity and the life cycle.* New York: W.W. Norton.

"While parenting and many professions provide such opportunities. . ." Josselson, R. (2017). *Paths to fulfillment: Women's search for meaning and identity*. New York: Oxford University Press; Vaillant, G. (2003). *Aging well: Surprising guideposts to a happier life from the landmark Harvard study of adult development*. Boston: Little, Brown; Slater, C.L. (2003). Generativity versus stagnation: An elaboration of Erikson's adult stage of human development. *Journal of Adult Development 10*(1), 53-65.

"While two-thirds of Italian grandparents . . ." Pew Research Center (2015). Family support in graying societies. Retrieved from http://www.pewsocialtrends.org/2015/05/21/2-supporting-family-members/

"The impact of grandparent involvement on children..." Barnett, M.A., Scaramella, L.V., Neppl, T.K., Ontai, L.L., & Conger, R.D. (2010). Grandmother involvement as a protective factor for early childhood social adjustment. Journal of Family Psychology, 24, No. 5, 635–645; Griggs, J., Tan, J-P, Buchanan, A, Attar-Schwartz, S., & Flouri, E. (2010). 'They've always been there for me': Grandparental involvement and child well-being. *Children & Society, 24*, 200-214.

Chapter 7: How to be an Engaged Grandparent

"Noncustodial grandparents get time off as well as time on . . ." Craig, L., & Jenkins, B. (2016). The composition of parents' and grandparents' child-care time: Gender and generational patterns in activity, multi-tasking and co-presence. *Ageing & Society, 36*(4), 785-810.

"Active grandparents are in the moment . . ." Langer, E. J., Cohen, M., & Djikic, M. (2012). Mindfulness as a psychological attractor: The effect on children. *Journal of Applied Social Psychology, 42*(5), 1114-1122.

"As with most relationships . . ." Lakó, J. H. (2014). The issues of the relationship of grandparents and grandchildren in the light of physical activity. *European Journal of Mental Health, 9*(2), 178-194.

AFTERWORD

We hope that you have found the grandparent experiences described and the advice given to be helpful. Every grandparent - grandchild relationship has joys and challenges. For most, over the years, the connections are sustaining.

It is our hope that you and your grandchildren will cherish each other and form special bonds. If our book has helped you in specific ways or if you have some additional advice to share with us, please send us an email at grand.publications.10@gmail.com

ACKNOWLEDGEMENTS

Creating a book requires assistance, especially when it is based upon the lives of others. We are grateful to those who shared their grandparenting experiences with us, as well as to those who encouraged grandparents to do so. We were persistent -- and at times annoying -- as we invited grandparents we met to participate and reminded friends and acquaintances to respond. Thanks for putting up with us. For their exceptional support and help in recruiting grandparents, we thank: Judie Block, Mary Coles, Joanne and Michael Feldstein, Shirley Flint, Paula Foster, Elizabeth Mainiaro, Angela McKelvey, Tara Rothman and Dianne Weinfeld.

We also thank these important people who helped turn our manuscript into this book: Roger Clark, Deborah M. Garskof, and Elizabeth Mainiaro for thoughtful readings of the manuscript, Deborah M. Garskof for legal counsel, Barbara Kuebke for copyediting and formatting advice, Robin Lenowitz

129

for art direction and Lucy Baker for marketing and publicity.

Special thanks to George Adler and John Mack Faragher, our husbands and grandparenting partners, for their counsel and support along the way, to our adult children who made us grandparents, and to our grandchildren who have provided us with a rich variety of experiences and stories to share.

ABOUT THE AUTHORS

Emily Stier Adler, Ph.D. is Professor Emerita of Sociology at Rhode Island College. An engaging and popular professor, she continues to teach a gerontology course, the Sociology of Aging. Dr. Adler has been a research consultant in a number of settings and the director of Women's Studies at the college. Her published work includes five editions of the co-authored *An Invitation to Social Research: How It's Done* and *The Elect: Rhode Island's Women Legislators* as well as numerous articles. Her research has focused on marriage, teenage pregnancy, adolescence, political life, retirement and grandparenthood. Married for fifty years, with two adult children, Dr. Adler enjoys spending time with her family, especially her four active grandchildren.

Michele Hoffnung, Ph.D. is Professor Emerita of Psychology at Quinnipiac University. She developed the women's studies program and directed it for its first two decades. Her published work includes *Roles Women Play: Readings in Women's Liberation; What's a Mother to Do?*; several editions of the co-authored textbook *Lifespan Development*; and numerous articles about women's roles, women's choices, motherhood, and grandmotherhood. She has been honored with the Pioneer Award and the Society for the Psychology of Women Heritage Award, from the American Psychological Association for her contributions to feminist psychology, and was recently inducted to the Associate Alumnae of Douglass College Society of Excellence. She and her husband are parents of three adult children and grandparents to each of their two children.

Photo Credits

Introduction: S.G. Aucoin

Chapter 1: C. Maynard on unsplash,
E. S. Adler, L. Rivas on unsplash

Chapter 2: M. Hoffnung, A. Seaman on unsplash,
H. Lee on unsplash

Chapter 3: M. Price on unsplash,
D. Macinnes on unsplash, L. Scout on unsplash

Chapter 4: S. Dixon on unsplash ,
E.S. Adler, A. Samoylova on unsplash

Chapter 5: F. Mckenna on unsplash,
J. Hoffnung-Garskof, V. Nordli-Mathisen on unsplash

Chapter 6: M. Hoffnung, S. Libralon on unsplash,
M. Hoffnung

Chapter 7: J Hoffnung-Garskof, N. Bariani on unsplash,
B. Hershey on unsplash

Chapter 8: E.S. Adler, A. Dummer on unsplash,
E.S. Adler